This book is full of
JOYFUL MOMENTS
we can make *together.*

To:_____

From:_____

Little Chef™

MY Very FIRST COOKBOOK

JOYFUL RECIPES to make together!

Recipes by
DANIELLE KARTES

Pictures by
ANNIE WILKINSON

sourcebooks
eXplore

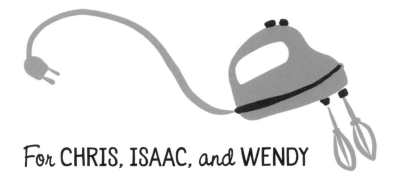

For CHRIS, ISAAC, and WENDY

Conversions

Oven Temperatures

Fahrenheit	Celsius	Gas Mark
275°	135°	1
300°	150°	2
325°	165°	3
350°	175°	4
375°	190°	5
400°	205°	6
425°	220°	7
450°	230°	8
475°	245°	9

US to Metric

cup	tablespoon	teaspoon	metric
1 c	16 tbsp	48 tsp	240 ml
3/4 c	12 tbsp	36 tsp	175 ml
2/3 c	10 tbsp + 2 tsp	32 tsp	160 ml
1/2 c	8 tbsp	24 tsp	120 ml
1/3 c	5 tbsp + 1 tsp	16 tsp	80 ml
1/4 c	4 tbsp	12 tsp	60 ml
1/8 c	2 tbsp	6 tsp	30 ml
1/16 c	1 tbsp	3 tsp	15 ml
--	--	1 tsp	5 ml

Text © 2020 by Danielle Kartes · Illustrations by Annie Wilkinson · Cover and internal design © 2020 by Sourcebooks · Sourcebooks, Little Chef, and the colophon are registered trademarks of Sourcebooks. · All rights reserved. · Published by Sourcebooks eXplore, an imprint of Sourcebooks Kids · P.O. Box 4410, Naperville, Illinois 60567-4410 · (630) 961-3900 · sourcebookskids.com · Source of Production: 1010 Printing Asia Limited, North Point, Hong Kong, China · Date of Production: November 2020 · Run Number: 5020263 · Printed and bound in China. · OGP 10 9 8 7 6 5 4 3 2

WHAT'S on the MENU?

In this book, you'll find simple, delicious recipes for you and a parent, grandparent, or big brother or sister to make together. Each recipe includes ways to personalize it. Do you love strawberries more than blueberries? No problem! Make pancakes with strawberry syrup. This is your special time together with your family and friends. Use what you love or whatever you have on hand!

BREAKFAST

LUNCH

SNACK

Almond Butter Dip with Apples and Pretzels ★ 28

Cheesy Jammy Toaster Waffles ★ 29

Cinnamon Sugar Popcorn ★ 30

Superstar Guacamole ★ 31

Fruity Fruity Strawberry Fruit Dip ★ 32

Crunchy Fried Pickles with Tasty Comeback Sauce ★ 34

Yogurt and Granola Parfaits ★ 36

Crunchy Veggies and Buttermilk Ranch Dip ★ 37

BEVERAGE

Fresh-Squeezed Lemonade ★ 38

Mean Green Fruity Smoothie ★ 39

Strawberry and Orange Slushy ★ 40

Creamy Soda Fountain Egg Creams ★ 41

DINNER

Sheet Pan Fajitas ★ 42

Sizzling Beef and Broccoli ★ 44

Chicken Meatball Sliders ★ 46

French Dip Sandwiches ★ 48

Chicken Tortellini Soup ★ 49

Inside-Out Creamy Stuffed Shells with Turkey and Broccoli ★ 50

Simply Swedish Meatballs with Mashers ★ 52

Chicky Tortilla Roll-Ups ★ 54

SIDES

DESSERTS

BONUS DELICIOUSNESS

Making Joyful
MEMORIES TOGETHER

Cooking along with a loved one will help you both to create new and wonderful traditions together! Here are some ways you can make your time in the kitchen special.

★ Do you like to listen to music? Pick a fun song you and your grown-up helper enjoy that can be played each time you cook together.

★ Try wearing matching aprons, chef's hats, or shirts!

★ Work together to decide who gets to collect what, who gets to crack the eggs, and who gets to taste test as you cook!

★ Use a special mixing bowl or spoon that can only be used when you're working in the kitchen together.

★ Eat your food on fancy dishes (if you want to)!

Follow these **SUPER** important steps to be the **VERY BEST** chef in town!

1. Listen well to instructions.
Cooking together is fun, but remember that an adult cares for you and knows what's best, so listen close at every step!

2. Wash your hands.
Clean hands make sure that no germy germs or greasy griminess make their way into your food.

3. Keep a clean workspace.
The best chefs pick up all clutter and wipe down the countertops as they work. Ask an adult for a clean, damp dishcloth to get started!

4. Never touch knives without permission.
A grown-up will be a big help if any food needs to be chopped!

5. Keep hands and arms away from hot ovens, boiling pots, and sizzling stoves.
This way you won't get burned, and it gives an adult a chance to help you by turning the heat up or down!

Best-Ever BUTTERMILK BLUEBERRY MUFFINS

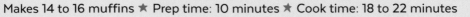

Makes 14 to 16 muffins ★ Prep time: 10 minutes ★ Cook time: 18 to 22 minutes

Before we get started, the very first thing you MUST do is wash your hands. Then it's muffin time!

Equipment

Muffin tin liners
Muffin tin
Large mixing bowl
Wooden spoon

Ingredients

½ cup salted butter, softened
1 cup granulated sugar
2 tablespoons olive oil
2 eggs, room temperature
    (If your egg isn't room
    temperature, place it in a cup
    of warm water for one minute.)
1¾ cups all-purpose flour
1 teaspoon baking powder
1 teaspoon kosher salt OR
    ½ teaspoon any other salt
½ teaspoon baking soda
1 cup buttermilk
1 teaspoon vanilla extract
1 tablespoon flour
2 cups fresh blueberries
    (frozen work too)

1. Ask an adult to preheat oven to 350°F and place muffin tin liners into your muffin tin.

2. Let's mix up our ingredients! Place butter, sugar, and olive oil into your mixing bowl and give it all a big stir. This part may be a little tough to get going, but you can do it! Of course, you can ask for can help too. Stir until the mixture is fluffy and well combined. This is called "creaming" the butter and sugar!

3. Now "incorporate" the eggs by cracking them into the bowl and stir just until you can't see the eggs anymore.

4. Add the dry ingredients to your bowl and gently mix it up. It sure is fun to stir, but try not to overmix because we want the muffins to be tender and fluffy!

5. Add the buttermilk and vanilla, then give the mixture just a little stir.

6. Sprinkle one tablespoon of flour over the blueberries. This keeps the blueberries from sinking to the bottom of the muffin. Stir the blueberries into the batter. Remember: just barely mix it. Now you are finally ready to fill your muffin cups!

7. Fill the muffin cups just a little over halfway. This gives the muffin room to grow in the oven. No overflowing muffins on your watch! (But if they do, it's OK!)

8. Stand back and let an adult put the muffins into the hot oven. Bake 12 to 18 minutes or until the muffins are lightly golden and nicely puffed up.

No muffin tin? Make a cake! Generously butter and flour a 9-x-13 baking dish and bake 22 to 28 minutes or until the cake is completely cooked and lightly golden.

Substitute 2 cups of raspberries or chopped strawberries for the blueberries or try a combination.

No muffin liners? No worries! Generously butter and flour your muffin tin.

For double chocolate muffins, replace ½ cup flour with ½ cup cocoa powder, and add 2 cups chocolate chips in place of the blueberries.

CINNAMON SWIRL FRENCH TOAST
with PINEAPPLE MAPLE SYRUP

Makes 12 slices ★ Prep time: 5 minutes ★ Cook time: 15 minutes

Pull up a chair or stool to the counter so you can help make the best breakfast EVER!

Equipment

Medium-size bowl

Wide shallow bowl

Whisk

Large skillet

Wide spatula for flipping

Ingredients

For the Syrup

1½ cups maple syrup

1 cup fresh pineapple, chopped

For the French Toast

1 (14- to 16-ounce) loaf cinnamon
   swirl bread (Stale bread works
   the very best!)

3 eggs

1 cup heavy cream or half-and-half
   (milk works just fine too)

½ teaspoon vanilla extract

½ teaspoon ground cinnamon

Pinch of salt

2 teaspoons butter for the pan,
   plus extra for smearing on
   the toast

1 Let's make the pineapple maple syrup! Mix the syrup and fruit together in your medium-size bowl and set aside.

2 If the loaf of bread is already sliced, skip ahead to step 3. If not, slice the bread equally into 12 one-inch-thick slices. This is a job for a grown-up, but don't worry—you are up next!

3 Crack the eggs into the wide shallow bowl. Don't be afraid, you are a professional egg cracker! If you happen to lose a bit of shell in the bowl, use a large piece of the shell to scoop out the tiny piece!

4 Add the cream, vanilla, cinnamon, and salt to the bowl, then whisk like the wind! Well, whisk like a gentle breeze...we don't want to spill.

5 Have an adult heat the skillet on medium heat. Melt 2 teaspoons of butter into the hot pan.

6 Dunk the bread into the egg custard and count to two out loud. Flip it over, dunk the other side, and count to two. Now it's ready for an adult to lay it on the pan. Can you hear the hot butter sizzle? It's going to taste so good!

7 Cook one side until golden brown (roughly 2 to 3 minutes), then flip! Cook for an additional 2 to 3 minutes on the other side.

8 Once your bread is all Frenchy and toasty and cooked, serve up each slice with a smear of butter and a spoonful (or two!) of your pineapple maple syrup.

No cinnamon bread? Perfectly fine! Use any bread you have, but remember: stale bread works best because it absorbs more custard.

Don't want to stand at the pan to fry every piece of toast? Preheat your oven to 375°F and generously butter a 9-by-13 pan. Then add the custard-soaked slices of bread to the pan and bake 20 to 25 minutes or until golden brown and puffed.

Substitute your favorite fruit for the pineapple in the syrup. Use blueberries or chopped strawberries! Bananas are delicious too!

No syrup? Smear on a little peanut butter or jam or a dusting of powdered sugar. Anything goes! Whipped cream sure loves French toast as well, so feel free to add some on top your toast!

Loaded HASH BROWNS

Makes 4 servings ★ Cook time: 10 to 15 minutes

Crispy, crunchy, delicious hash browns. They're like teeny tiny French fries all in a pile that you can eat for breakfast! Let's do it!

Equipment

Large skillet

Spatula

Ingredients

For the Hash Browns

2 tablespoons butter

2 tablespoons olive oil

1 (20- to 30-ounce) bag frozen hash browns

Salt and pepper to taste

For the Garnish

1 cup cheddar cheese, shredded

1 cup sour cream

1 cup bacon crumbles

½ cup green onions, chopped

1 Ask a grown-up to put the skillet on the stove and set the heat between medium and medium-high. Carefully add the butter and oil to the pan.

2 Sprinkle the frozen hash browns into the pan and fry until they are browned on one side, 5 to 7 minutes. Then, flip them over and brown them on the other side, 3 to 4 minutes.

3 Top crispy, warm hash browns with cheddar cheese, sour cream, bacon crumbles, and green onions!

Serve alongside fried or scrambled eggs.

Chop up sausages and fry them in the hash browns.

Crack several eggs into the crispy, almost-cooked hash browns for a tasty scramble!

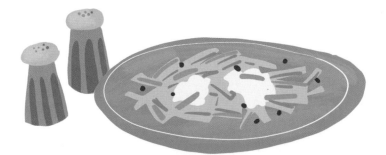

Apple Cinnamon OVERNIGHT OATS

Makes 4 servings ★ Prep time: 10 minutes + 8 hours chilling time

Right before bed, mix up a batch of these tasty no-cooking-required oats and enjoy a delicious breakfast in the morning!

Equipment

Large bowl or container
  with lid
Wooden spoon

Ingredients

1 cup rolled oats
1 apple, peeled, cored, and
  finely chopped
2 tablespoons brown
  sugar
¾ cup whole milk
¼ cup cream
½ teaspoon cinnamon
Pinch of salt

1 This is a magic recipe! All you need to do is mix everything up in a bowl or container with a tight-fitting lid and leave it in the refrigerator overnight! In the morning, you will have delicious apple cinnamon oatmeal to enjoy!

For a chocolate version, add 1 tablespoon cocoa powder and skip the apples!

Use any fruit you love!

Serve warm with a pat of butter by microwaving your portion 30 to 45 seconds.

Toads-in-the-Hole TOASTS

Makes 4 to 6 slices ★ Prep time: 5 minutes ★ Cook time: 15 minutes

This is one froggy breakfast you are sure to love! So let's wash those hands and pull up a chair. Who can resist buttery toast and cheesy eggs?

Equipment

1 (2.5- to 3-inch) cookie cutter, any shape
10- to 12-inch frying pan
Spatula
Plate

Ingredients

4 to 6 slices of bread
½ cup butter
4 to 6 eggs
1 cup cheddar cheese, shredded

1 Line up your bread slices on the counter and use the cookie cutter to cut a shape out of the middle of each slice. Save those cutout bits!

2 Ask an adult to turn the stove to medium and heat 1 tablespoon of the butter in the frying pan. Okay, kiddo, now you use your spatula to swirl the butter around the pan! Nice work! Lay one bread slice into the pan and lay the bread cutout next to it. Listen for a teeny tiny sizzle.

3 Take an egg and give it a gentle tap on the counter. Not too hard! Just enough to give the shell a nice crack. Use your fingers to open the shell, and carefully tip the egg into the hole in the bread on the pan. This might be tricky, so ask for help! Be sure to wash your hands! Fry the bread for 2 to 3 minutes or until the egg is set and not wobbly. Then ask your grown-up helper to help flip everything.

4 Sprinkle 2 tablespoons of cheese over the toasty bread cutout. Cook another 2 to 3 minutes.

5 Remove your eggy bread slice carefully from the pan and set on a plate, then top the eggy bit with your toasty, cheesy cutout.

6 Repeat these steps for all of your slices, and you've just made Toads-in-the-Hole Toasts! But shhhh...don't tell anyone it's just fancy, buttery, cheesy eggs and toast.

Use any style of bread or cheese you want!

Add a slice of ham on top before you add the bread cutout to make a breakfast sandwich!

Serve these up with ketchup or hot sauce for dunking.

Want a meaty side? Fry up breakfast sausages in the very same pan. Slice the sausages in half lengthwise for quicker cooking.

DROP SCONES with BUTTER and JAM

Alright, little chef, wash up and let's get started!

Equipment

Large mixing bowl
Wooden spoon
Parchment paper
Baking sheet
Spatula
Cooling rack

Ingredients

2¼ cups all-purpose flour
¼ cup sugar
1 tablespoon baking powder
½ cup plus 2 tablespoons
   cold butter, diced
½ teaspoon kosher salt
½ cup heavy cream
¼ cup buttermilk
Strawberry jam and butter
   for spreading once
   scones are baked

1 Ask an adult to preheat the oven to 375°F. Measure the flour, sugar, and baking powder into the mixing bowl, then mix the butter in until you've got little teeny tiny bits of butter. The mixture should look a bit like coarse sand or bread crumbs.

2 Add the salt, cream, and buttermilk and mix it up! It'll be sticky, so ask a grown-up to can help if your arm gets tired. Don't overmix. Stop stirring when the dough starts to stick together. Crumbly is ok!

3 Cut a sheet of parchment paper and place it on top of the baking sheet. This helps the scones not to stick to the pan. Spoon ¼ cup dollops of the batter onto your baking sheet and ask an adult to put the baking sheet in the oven. Bake 15 to 20 minutes, or until golden brown.

4 Remove the scones from the baking sheet to the cooling rack with your spatula. Then pick your favorite and slather up the warm scone with butter or jam or both! Oh boy, don't they look yummy!

Add 1 cup chocolate chips for chocolate chip scones!

If you'd like pumpkin scones, skip the buttermilk and add ¼ cup pumpkin purée plus ½ teaspoon cinnamon. These are great in the fall!

For you fruit lovers, add 1 cup diced fresh fruit such as strawberries, blackberries, or peaches to create a fun, fruity scone.

What's a scarecrow's favorite fruit?

Strawberries.

Hee-hee!

Ha-ha!

Ha-ha!

FLUFFY LEMON *and* RICOTTA PANCAKES *with* BLUEBERRY SYRUP

Makes 6 to 8 four-inch pancakes ★ Prep time: 10 minutes ★ Cook time: 10 to 15 minutes

Before you begin to cook any meal, make sure you wash those hands with soap and warm water. Now pull a chair or stool up to the counter so you can help, and let's begin!

Equipment

Large mixing bowl
½ cup measuring cup
Medium-size saucepan
12-inch nonstick skillet
Spatula

Ingredients

For the Pancakes

1 cup flour
1 cup whole milk or half-and-half
½ cup ricotta cheese
1 egg
2 tablespoons olive oil
2 tablespoons granulated sugar
2 teaspoons baking powder
½ teaspoon kosher salt
Zest and juice of one lemon
Butter for the pan and some
    for serving

For the Blueberry Syrup

2 cups fresh blueberries
¾ cup water
½ cup sugar

1 Have a grown-up help you measure out each of the pancake ingredients and dump them into the large mixing bowl. Stir, stir, stir! Stir the batter until mostly combined, with lumps the size of little pebbles throughout. Lumpy pancake batter makes the yummiest pancakes!

2 Ask a grown-up to turn on the stove to medium heat. Stand back! No funny business around the hot stove! Ask your helper to add some butter to the skillet and place over the heat. Here comes the best part! Use the measuring cup to scoop the batter from the bowl and pour it into the skillet. You should be able to fit three pancakes at a time. Watch for teeny-tiny bubbles to appear all over the top of the pancakes. That is when they are perfectly ready to flip! Tell your adult that it's time to use the spatula to carefully flip the pancakes and turn down the heat a little. Remove the pancakes from the skillet when both sides are golden brown. Repeat this process until you've used up all that batter! Remember, just a little butter in the hot skillet makes a crisp, buttery edge—the very tastiest part of the whole pancake!

3 While you are the fierce bubble hunter of the pancakes, have your grown-up helper begin cooking the blueberries in the saucepan. Boil the blueberries, water, and sugar over medium-high heat until those tiny berries begin to boogie and burst! It only takes about 10 minutes!

4 To serve up your beautiful breakfast, smear a little soft butter on a warm pancake and drizzle it with warm blueberry syrup!

No fresh blueberries? Frozen berries work great! In fact, you can make this dish with any frozen berry or even stone fruit like peaches, plums, or cherries.

Skip the lemon and dress the pancakes with maple syrup.

No ricotta? No problem! You can use plain yogurt or vanilla-flavored yogurt.

Add ½ cup chocolate chips to the batter! The chocolate is delicious with the citrus and blueberry.

Use another fresh fruit if you'd like! Raspberries and strawberries work beautifully.

SOFT SCRAMBLED *Cheesy* EGGS

Makes 4 servings ★ Prep time: 5 minutes ★ Cook time: 10 minutes

Eggs are delicious when you cook them slowly over a low heat! You will be making the best cheesy eggs you've ever tasted!

Equipment

Large nonstick skillet
Silicone spatula

Ingredients

1 tablespoon butter
10 eggs
½ cup heavy cream
Salt and pepper to taste
1 cup cheddar cheese, shredded

1 Put the skillet on the stove and ask an adult to turn the heat between low and medium. Add the butter and let it get all melty and a little sizzle-y!

2 Crack the eggs into the pan. This can be tricky, but be confident! A quick tap on the countertop cracks the shell just enough for you to push your thumb into the hole and separate the shell into halves. If a shell fragment falls in, it's okay—use a big piece of shell to scoop out the tiny piece.

3 Gently stir with the spatula until the eggs are mixed up, but not fully! You want little ribbons of white through the cooked scramble. Now, add the cream, salt, and pepper. Stir.

4 After about 5 minutes, when the eggs look glossy, sprinkle on the cheese. Cook a minute or two longer, or until they look firm and not runny, with a little shine on top. Smash them on top of toast or even a baked potato!

Add some tender, young greens such as spinach or arugula.

Some hot sauce at the end is DELICIOUS if you are a spice-lovin' kiddo!

Add leftover cooked sausage or ham to the pan at the very beginning!

Cooking brings out the very best in everyone. When you feed people you love, they feel that love from you! They can see and taste how much you care for them by the way you prepare delicious dishes for them. Good food makes everyone happy! Enjoy spending this time with each other as you make these fun, simple, joyful recipes.

Why do eggs hate jokes?

Because they always crack up!

Hee-hee!

Ha-ha!

Easy-Peasy TOMATO SOUP and TOASTED TRIPLE CHEESE SAMMIES

Makes 2 quarts of soup and 4 sandwiches ★ Prep time: 10 minutes ★ Cook time: 20 minutes

Equipment

Stock pot

Large mixing bowl

Stick blender or traditional blender

Frying pan

Spatula

Plate

Ladle (if using a traditional blender)

Ingredients

For the Soup

4 tablespoons butter

1 medium yellow onion, roughly chopped

1 (28-ounce) can whole peeled tomatoes in juice

3 fresh tomatoes, chopped

4 cups low-sodium chicken stock or broth

3 cloves garlic, smashed

½ cup sweet basil, chopped

Salt and pepper to taste

½ cup heavy cream

For the Sammies

8 ounces cream cheese, softened

2 cups cheddar cheese, shredded

1 cup mozzarella, shredded

Salt and pepper to taste

½ teaspoon onion powder

8 slices of bread

Butter for the pan

1 Set your stock pot on the stove. Add the butter and ask an adult to turn the heat to medium. Once the butter is melted, add the onion. Cook until the onions are translucent—that means a little see-through! Add the rest of the soup ingredients except the cream, and simmer for 20 minutes.

2 While the soup simmers, put the cheeses, salt, pepper, and onion powder into a bowl and mash it up with a fork. Ask an adult to heat the frying pan up to medium heat.

3 Spread a little butter on the outsides of two bread slices, then spread your cheese mixture gently on the inside. Repeat this process until you have four sammies! You are a toasted cheese sammie machine!

4 With a grown-up's help, put one sammie in the pan. Cook one side until it's crispy and the cheese is melting, then flip and do the same on the other side! Remove from the pan and set aside on a plate.

5 Ask an adult to remove the soup from the heat. Blend 2 to 3 minutes with the stick blender in the pot, or ask a grown-up to carefully ladle the soup into a blender. Once it's smooth and ready for dunking, pour the soup back into the pot. Add heavy cream and stir it up. Serve your soup with the toasted triple cheese sammies, and you are in for a delish lunch!

No blender? No problem! Swap out the can of whole tomatoes for crushed tomatoes, and serve up a chunky tomato soup.

Skip the grilled cheese and add cooked tortellini to the soup.

Gluten free? This will work great with your very favorite gluten-free bread!

Add any cheese you have to the cheese mixture!

Want the soup dairy free? Use olive oil instead of butter and skip the heavy cream.

Add any cooked ground meat to the soup and skip the blender for a hearty stew.

Waffle PIZZA SAMMIES

Makes 4 sandwiches ★ Prep time: 10 minutes ★ Cook time: 20 minutes

**Everybody loves waffles, right? And everybody loves pizza!
What if you could make a waffle-shaped pizza sandwich?
You can! Wash those hands and pull up your stool!**

Equipment

2 small bowls
Waffle iron
Cooling rack

Ingredients

8 slices sandwich bread
1 (7-ounce) package sliced
    pepperoni
8 slices deli mozzarella
½ cup (1 stick) butter,
    softened
2 cups marinara sauce

1 Have a grown-up turn the waffle iron on to medium heat.

2 Assemble your sammies! Gently spread butter on one side of each slice of bread. Flip 4 slices of bread buttered side down and layer on the mozzarella, pepperoni, more mozzarella, and top with another slice of bread (buttered side up).

3 Waffle time! Ask an adult to will place the sandwiches one at a time into the waffle iron. Don't touch the hot waffle iron! You will hear sizzles and crackles as the bread toasts and your waffle pizza sandwich is made. Once all four sandwiches are cooked (about 6 to 10 minutes), ask an adult to move the sammies from the hot waffle iron to the cooling rack. We're almost ready for a really yummy lunch!

4 Pour ½ cup marinara per sandwich into a small dish for dipping your crispy, delicious pizza sammie.

No pepperoni? No problem! Skip it or use cooked crumbled sausage, sautéed veggies, or leftover rotisserie chicken!

No marinara for dunking? Perfectly fine! Ranch dressing is yummy for dipping, and so is sour cream! Not a dunker? That's okay too! Plain is perfect!

Serve these not-so-traditional waffle pizza sandwiches alongside tomato soup for a deliciously different take on the classic grilled cheese sandwich!

Mini CORN DOG BITES

Makes 20 corn dogs ★ Prep time: 10 minutes ★ Cook time: 10 to 15 minutes

Equipment

Large saucepan
20 extra-long toothpicks
Large mixing bowl
Wooden spoon
Paper towels
Large plate

Ingredients

4 cups oil suitable for frying
(The best oils for frying
are olive or coconut oil,
but canola or vegetable oil
work too!)
20 little smoky sausages
(roughly half of a 14-ounce
package)
1 cup buttermilk
½ cup cornmeal
½ cup flour
¼ cup sugar
¼ cup butter, melted
1 egg
2 teaspoons baking powder
½ teaspoon kosher salt

1. Ask a grown-up to heat the oil in the saucepan over medium heat while you stick a toothpick into each sausage!

2. Put the rest of the ingredients in the mixing bowl and stir them up to make the batter.

3. By now the oil should be nice and hot and almost shimmering. Only an adult should handle the hot pan! Dunk each hot dog into the batter and CAREFULLY drop each one into the hot oil. Fry 3 to 4 minutes or until they're golden brown. Remove and set aside on a paper towel–covered plate until cool.

If you can't find mini hot dogs, cut 5 regular hot dogs into 4 pieces each.

Add hot sauce to the batter for extra spiciness!

Set up a dipping bar with ketchup, mustard, or even ranch dip! Whatever you like to dunk into!

Veggie FRIED RICE

Makes 4 servings ★ Prep time: 5 minutes ★ Cook time: 15 minutes

Equipment

Small bowl
Large nonstick skillet
Wooden spoon

Ingredients

For the Sauce

⅓ cup soy sauce
1 tablespoon brown sugar
1 teaspoon mustard
1 garlic clove, smashed
    and chopped

For the Rice

2 tablespoons olive oil
2½ cups rice, cooked
2 cups veggies of your
    choice (Think carrots
    and onions, snap peas,
    or broccoli. A mixture
    is great! Use what
    you have.)
1 egg

1 Mix up the ingredients for the sauce in a small bowl and set aside.

2 Put the skillet on the stove and have an adult crank the heat up to medium-high. Pour the oil into the pan and let it heat up. Add the rice and veggies. Cook 4 to 5 minutes.

3 Make a well in the center of the rice and crack the egg into the pan, stirring gently but quickly to scramble the egg.

4 Pour the sauce into the rice. Cook 2 to 3 minutes and serve!

Add chopped cucumbers and peanuts at the end for a delightful crunch!

Add 1 cup of any leftover cooked meat you have in the fridge.

Veggies are yummy!

Skip the sauce if you like it plain.

Stovetop MAC 'N' CHEESE

Makes 4 servings ★ Prep time: 10 minutes ★ Cook time: 10 minutes

No boxed macaroni and cheese over here! I bet you have everything to make this in your refrigerator and pantry. This is as cheesy and simple and yummy as it gets, friend. Wash those hands and pull up a chair!

Equipment

Stockpot

Wooden spoon

Cheese grater

Ingredients

12 ounces dry elbow pasta

8 ounces cheddar cheese, shredded

1 tablespoon butter

1 cup heavy cream

Salt and pepper to taste

1 Fill the pot with 2 quarts of water and have an adult put it on the stove to boil. You will need high heat for this! Cook the pasta according to the package's instructions, or until just soft enough to bite into. This is called *al dente*, from the Italian word for "tooth"!

2 When the noodles are done, ask a grown-up to help you to drain them. Next, you put the super delicious cheese, butter, and cream into the pot! Careful, the pan is very hot. Now stir, stir, stir! Once it's all melty, it's ready!

Try to use cheddar cheese shredded off the block. Pre-shredded cheese has a powder on it that can make your mac 'n' cheese a little gritty and not so smooth.

Add 1 cup frozen peas along with the cheese.

Add 1 cup leftover chili to make chili mac, or simply add cooked ground beef for a protein-packed lunch.

Serve alongside sliced apples and snap peas for a fun, crunchy, healthy side dish.

Cook fresh broccoli in the same pot as you are cooking the noodles for broccoli mac 'n' cheese.

Use up any other cheese you have on hand. Mozzarella, Parmesan, and Swiss all make lovely additions to the cheddar.

WARM and TOASTY HAM and CHEESE ROLLS

Makes 4 servings ★ Prep time: 10 minutes

Equipment

Baking sheet
Parchment paper
Small bowl
Spoon or rubber spatula

Ingredients

4 bread rolls, sliced in half
1 tablespoon mustard
¼ cup mayonnaise
12 ounces sliced deli ham
4 slices cheddar cheese

1 Preheat the oven to 375°F with an adult's help. Cover the baking sheet with a sheet of parchment paper.

2 In the small bowl, mix the mustard and mayo together and spread just a bit on the inside of every roll. Divide the ham and cheese among the four rolls.

3 Place the sandwiches on the baking sheet, and ask a grown-up to put them in the oven. Bake 10 to 15 minutes until the cheese is nice and melty and that roll is oh-so-toasty! Ask an adult to take the rolls out of the oven, and serve alongside crunchy chips and sliced veggies such as carrot sticks and peapods!

Use any bread, cheese, or meat you like!

Top your sammies with crunchy pickles, lettuce, or tomato!

Turkey PINWHEELS

Makes 12 pinwheels ★ Prep time: 10 minutes

This one's easy-peasy to make and eat!

Equipment

Plate
Knife

Ingredients

4 flour tortillas (about 7 inches wide)

8 tablespoons cream cheese, softened

8 slices deli turkey meat

4 dill pickle slices

1 Lay out the tortillas and spread 2 tablespoons of cream cheese over each.

2 Lay 2 turkey slices and 1 pickle slice in the center of each tortilla.

3 Roll 'em up and slice each into 3 pieces. Arrange your pretty pinwheels on a plate and enjoy!

Add spinach and tomato slices for an extra serving of veggies!

Try a whole wheat or tomato-flavored tortilla to make it super tasty!

Use any deli meat you like. Ham would work great!

Chili Chili Chili DOGS

Makes 4 servings ★ Prep time: 10 minutes ★ Cook time: 45 minutes

Watch out chili champs, there's a new contender in town! This chili is so fast and easy that you can whip it up for lunch or dinner anytime!

Equipment

Large stock pot
Frying pan
Wooden spoon
Knife

Ingredients

For the Chili

1 medium yellow onion, chopped
1 bell pepper (any color), chopped
1 pound ground beef (85% lean)
2 teaspoons chili powder
1 teaspoon kosher salt
1 teaspoon onion powder
1 teaspoon paprika
½ teaspoon black pepper
½ teaspoon ground cumin
1 (15-ounce) can tomato sauce
1 cup chicken or beef stock
1 (15-ounce) can red kidney beans, drained
4 hot dogs
4 hot dog buns

For the Toppings

2 cups cheddar cheese, shredded
1 cup baby dill pickles
1 cup tomato, chopped
½ cup onions, diced finely

1 Set a nice big pot on the stove top and a frying pan right beside it. Have a grown-up turn on the heat under the pot to between medium and medium-high. Add the chopped onion, bell pepper, and ground beef to the big pot. Cook until the meat is browned and fully cooked, about 7 to 10 minutes.

2 Add the seasonings, tomato sauce, stock, and beans and stir it up gently with a wooden spoon. Now let the chili simmer on low heat for about 30 minutes. That's it! All this simmering helps the chili to taste amazing!

3 Let's fry up those weenies! Cut the hot dogs in half lengthwise and have a grown-up cook them in a frying pan over medium-high heat. This only takes 3 to 4 minutes.

4 Put two halves of hot dog slices into a hot dog bun and fill with chili. Then add any other delicious toppings you'd like. This is the most fun part! Don't skimp on the cheese!

Use any ground meat you want, or skip the meat altogether and add 1 more can of drained kidney beans.

Use leftover chili for nachos or sloppy joe-style sandwiches.

No seasonings on hand? Use a chili seasoning packet. It's affordable and easy.

ALMOND BUTTER DIP with APPLES and PRETZELS

Makes a little under 1 cup ★ Prep time: 5 minutes

Equipment
Medium-size bowl
Spoon for mixing
Plate

Ingredients
½ cup almond butter
¼ cup half-and-half
2 tablespoons honey
¼ teaspoon cinnamon
Salt to taste
2 apples
1 cup pretzel sticks

1 Stir the almond butter, half-and-half, honey, and cinnamon in your bowl. Then with your clean pointer finger, have a taste and ask an adult to help you with how much salt to add. "To taste" means you get to decide!

2 Slice the apples up, then you can arrange them on a plate with the pretzel sticks. Try a fun design! Then dig into your delicious dip and enjoy!

For chocolate almond butter dip, add 1 tablespoon unsweetened cocoa powder.

Makes a delicious addition to buttered toast.

Dip bananas or celery for fun twist!

CHEESY *Jammy* TOASTER WAFFLES

Makes 2 servings ★ Prep time: 5 minutes

This is the most fun! It sounds like a funny idea, but wait till you try it!

Equipment

Toaster

Ingredients

4 frozen waffles

2 tablespoons blackberry jam

2 slices cheddar cheese

1 Pop the waffles into the toaster.

2 When they pop up, spread 1 tablespoon of jam on one side and cover it with a slice of cheese!

3 Top it with another waffle and **VOILÀ!** You've got a cheesy, jammy, waffle sammy!

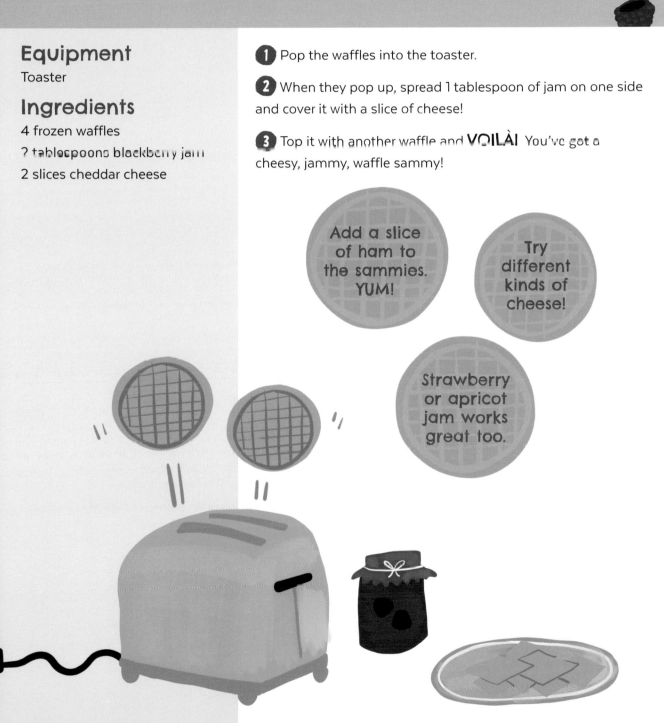

Add a slice of ham to the sammies. YUM!

Try different kinds of cheese!

Strawberry or apricot jam works great too.

Cinnamon Sugar POPCORN

Makes 4 cups ★ Prep time: 6 minutes

Equipment

Large bowl
Small bowl

Ingredients

1 bag plain microwave
    popcorn
1 tablespoon butter, melted
¼ teaspoon cinnamon
1 tablespoon granulated sugar

1 Ask a grown-up to follow the microwave popcorn instructions while you stir the cinnamon and sugar together.

2 Once the popcorn is popped, pour it into a nice big bowl (careful, it's hot!) and drizzle that melted butter all over the top! Then sprinkle on the cinnamon sugar.

3 Sit somewhere with your grown-up helper and ask for their favorite stories about when they were little. Or make a list of each of your favorite movies and watch them together! Popcorn makes everyone happy!

Superstar GUACAMOLE

Makes 4 servings ★ Prep time: 10 minutes

Do you love guacamole? This is super-duper easy, crazy tasty, and so much fun to make! You get to smash and stir up the most amazing dip and spread. Let's do it!

Equipment

Knife
Spoon
Mixing bowl
Fork

Ingredients

3 ripe avocados
1 tablespoon fresh lime juice
1 tablespoon fresh lemon juice
   (Lemon juice keeps
   guacamole from turning
   brown longer than lime
   juice does!)
¼ teaspoon garlic powder
¼ teaspoon onion powder
Kosher salt to taste
1 Roma tomato
¼ cup fresh cilantro,
   chopped
Tortilla chips

1. Ask an adult to slice all three avocados in half and take the big pits out. You get to scoop all the green fruit out of the bumpy skins into your bowl.

2. Measure out the lemon juice and lime juice. This gives the guacamole a yummy citrus flavor and keeps it from getting brown! Measure out the garlic powder, onion powder, and a pinch of salt into the bowl, then mash the avocado gently. Taste test! See if it needs more salt or other seasoning while your adult helper chops the tomato and cilantro.

3. Have your helper add the tomatoes and cilantro to the bowl, and you can gently mix them in. That's it! You are ready to dive in with some crispy tortilla chips!

> Don't like cilantro? Just skip it!

> Guacamole is amazing on sandwiches and in omelets!

> Love spicy? Add one small jalapeño, seeds and ribs removed, chopped.

Fruity Fruity STRAWBERRY FRUIT DIP

Makes roughly 2½ cups ★ Prep time: 10 minutes

Some combinations are almost too good to be true: cream cheese and honey, fruit and this dip, and your family and you! Now you can have all three at once. Make this dip and be thankful for all the perfect combos in your life.

Equipment

Hand mixer

Mixing bowl

Spoon or rubber spatula (optional)

Serving bowl (optional)

Ingredients

8 ounces cream cheese, softened

1 cup heavy cream

½ cup strawberries, chopped

2 tablespoons honey, or more if you'd like it sweeter

You can pick just one fruit or all the fun fruits to dip! Here are some fruits that love to be dunked:

Apples

Bananas, peeled

Strawberries

Orange segments

Grapes

Pears

1 Grab a hand mixer, the best mixer of all (well, besides you and your helper—you two might be the best mixers of ALL time)! Add the cream cheese, cream, strawberries, and honey to a large mixing bowl. Start your mixer on low speed. If it's a little heavy, ask an adult to help you steady the bowl and mixer. As the mixture mixes, it will start to get fluffy. The heavy cream is turning to whipped cream! Mix this until its light and fully whipped and you can't see any chunks of cream cheese. It should be nice and smooth!

2 Use a spoon or rubber spatula to move the dip into a serving bowl, or you can just leave it in the bigger bowl—no problem!

3 The final step is to use your clean pointer finger for a taste test! Remember, no double dipping! Does it need anything? Now is the time to add more honey or fruit or cream.

No strawberries? No problem! Use any juicy berry you have: blackberries, blueberries, or even raspberries work great!

Want a chocolate dip? Add ¼ cup hazelnut spread and 1 tablespoon unsweetened cocoa powder to the original recipe. Delicious!

No heavy cream? Well, fruit-flavored yogurt works wonderfully! Simply put an 8-ounce container of your favorite yogurt in with the cream cheese. It won't be as fluffy, but it's super yummy.

Don't want to dunk anymore? Chop up the fruit you have, and mix it together with the dip! This makes the yummiest fruit salad!

Crunchy FRIED PICKLES with Tasty COMEBACK SAUCE

Makes 4 servings ★ Prep time: 15 minutes ★ Cook time: 15 minutes

Have you ever heard of such a thing? Fried pickles are crispy and salty and crunchy and perfect for dunking! You know what to do—wash those hands and get up to the counter.

Equipment

Medium-size bowl

Medium-size saucepan

Plate

Paper towels

Whisk

Mixing bowl

Tongs

Slotted spoon

Ingredients

For the Sauce

¾ cup mayo

¼ cup ketchup

¼ cup dill pickle relish

¼ teaspoon onion power

For the Pickles

4 cups vegetable oil for frying

1 (16-ounce) jar sliced pickles

1 cup flour

1 teaspoon baking powder

1 cup seltzer water or club soda

½ teaspoon onion powder

¼ teaspoon kosher salt

¼ teaspoon cracked black pepper

Sea salt to taste

1 Mix up all the ingredients for the sauce in a medium-size bowl and set it in the fridge. You want the flavors to have plenty of time to get all happy together!

2 Add the oil to the saucepan and ask a grown-up to heat over medium-high. You should stand back because hot oil sometimes splashes a bit, and it gets very, very hot!

3 Drain the pickles and lay them on a few paper towels to soak up the extra liquid from the jar.

4 In a mixing bowl, whisk up the flour, baking powder, seltzer, and seasonings. Now have your helper make sure the oil is hot enough. It should be shimmering but not smoking.

5 Dunk the pickles into the batter, then have a grown-up use the tongs to carefully lay each pickle into the hot oil. This part can be tricky and tongs will help protect his hands. Load up the pan with at least 10 batter-dipped pickle chips at a time. Once the pickles are sizzling and golden brown, remove from the oil with the slotted spoon and set the fried pickles onto fresh paper towels. Sprinkle them with sea salt right away!

6 Repeat this process until you've used up all your pickles. Remove the sauce from the fridge, and now, little one, dunk the pickles in your sauce and enjoy!

Use all kinds of veggies! Green beans, broccoli, even pepperoni slices are a blast to fry.

Try adding a fried pickle to your favorite sandwich or even atop a yummy salad!

This makes delicious, crunchy fried chicken batter as well.

Not a dipper? Not a problem! These crunchy pickles taste great without sauce.

YOGURT and GRANOLA PARFAITS

Makes 2½ cups granola (4 servings) ★ Prep time: 10 minutes ★ Bake time: 15 minutes

Equipment

Large mixing bowl
Wooden spoon
Parchment paper
Baking sheet

Ingredients

For the Granola

2¼ cups rolled oats
¼ cup light-tasting oil
    (like canola)
¼ cup brown sugar
1 tablespoon butter, melted
1 teaspoon vanilla
¼ teaspoon ground cinnamon
Pinch of salt

For the Parfait

2 cups yogurt
2 cups fresh berries
Honey for drizzling

1 Ask your helper to turn the oven on to 350°F. Remember, never touch the oven without a grown-up's help.

2 Add all the granola ingredients to your large mixing bowl and stir them up! That's it, all done!

3 Now, pour the fresh granola out onto a parchment paper–lined baking sheet. Have your helper put the granola into the oven. Set a timer for 15 minutes. Voilà! Your granola is ready! After your helper takes it out of the oven, let it cool until the pan is no longer hot, hot, hot!

4 To make your parfait, put a little yogurt in a bowl or glass and make layers of granola, berries, honey, and more yogurt, if you'd like! Be creative!

For chocolate granola, add 1 tablespoon cocoa powder to the oats.

Sprinkle your granola on top of ice cream for a tasty, sweet crunch!

Enjoy your fresh granola with milk for breakfast!

Add the fresh granola to your favorite chocolate chip cookie recipe!

Add ½ cup sliced almonds for a nutty surprise!

CRUNCHY VEGGIES and BUTTERMILK RANCH DIP

★ Makes a little over 1 cup ★

Have you ever heard of "dump-and-stir" recipes? Simply dump the ingredients in a bowl, stir it up, and you have an easy, yummy dip! Serve with sugar snap peas, carrot sticks, broccoli, or cauliflower florets—or whatever you choose! It's all delicious!

Equipment

Mixing bowl

Fork or whisk for stirring

Ingredients

½ cup mayonnaise

½ cup sour cream

2 to 3 tablespoons buttermilk

½ teaspoon onion powder

½ teaspoon garlic powder

1 teaspoon dried chives

½ teaspoon dried thyme

¼ teaspoon dried rosemary

Salt and pepper to taste

2 to 3 cups of your favorite vegetables

1 Put all ingredients except the veggies into a mixing bowl and stir it up. You are now ready to dunk!

Add a little salsa for a kick.

Add a touch of hot sauce for some spice.

Add ¼ cup dill pickle relish and ¼ cup ketchup, and you've got a tasty thousand island dressing for salads or burgers!

Fresh-Squeezed LEMONADE

Makes 1 quart (4 cups) ★ Prep time: 15 minutes

Roll up those sleeves and get ready for the squeeze!

Equipment

2-quart pitcher
Wooden spoon
Citrus squeezer

Ingredients

4 to 6 lemons, juiced
1 cup granulated sugar
3 to 4 cups water

1 Wash those lemons with a good rinse under warm water. The warm water loosens up all those juices.

2 Ask an adult to cut each lemon in half. Squeeze 1 cup of lemon juice using your preferred squeezer, and pour it into your pitcher. Add the sugar and stir until it's dissolved, then add the water. Taste test! Add more water if it's too strong, more sugar if it's too sour, or more lemon juice if it's too sweet! Once it's perfect, enjoy!

Use this same recipe for limeade!

Smash ½ cup of raspberries into the lemon juice and sugar for a raspberry pink lemonade.

Add scoops of vanilla ice cream to your glass for a creamy lemonade float!

Mean Green FRUITY SMOOTHIE

Makes 4 (8-ounce) smoothies ★ Prep time: 5 minutes

Equipment
Blender

Ingredients
2 cups baby spinach

1 cup pineapple chunks

1 cup strawberries

1 ripe banana

1 cup yogurt

½ cup ice

½ cup apple juice or
    pineapple juice

1 Put all the ingredients in the blender. Then ask an adult to carefully turn it on. That's it! Smoothies are so much fun because you can make wildly different flavors just by using what you have.

The possibilities are endless! No spinach? No worries—use avocado or another baby green such as kale!

Use any berries you have, even frozen for a frosty treat!

For a chocolate peanut butter smoothie, put the banana, yogurt, and ice in the blender with ½ cup milk, ¼ cup peanut butter, and 1 tablespoon cocoa powder!

STRAWBERRY and ORANGE SLUSHY

Makes 4 servings ★ Prep time: 5 minutes

This is THE BEST! Slushy, slushy time! Pull up a chair and have a grown-up grab the blender and lid.

Equipment

Blender

Ingredients

2 cups ripe strawberries, tops removed

1 cup ice

2 cups orange juice

1 tablespoon lemon juice

1 to 2 tablespoons honey

1 Everything on the list goes into the blender! Put the lid on and ask an adult to help you turn the blender on. It's gonna get loud! Blend the ingredients up until nice and frosty smooth. Next, pour into cups and enjoy! Easy, right?!

Frozen fruit works great too!

Use any fruit juice you have.

No honey? No problem. Just skip it!

Creamy Soda Fountain EGG CREAMS

Makes 2 (8-ounce) smoothies ★ Prep time: 5 minutes

Guess what? Egg creams don't really have eggs. They're bubbly drinks made famous by 1950s diners—and delicious enough to drink today!

Equipment

2 tall (12-ounce) glasses
Tall, skinny spoon
2 straws

Ingredients

½ cup chocolate syrup
2 cups (16 ounces) club soda
½ cup heavy cream
2 maraschino cherries
1 can whipped cream (you will have lots leftover)

1 Squirt chocolate syrup in each glass, then add the ice.

2 Slowly pour the bubbly club soda into the glass. Leave an inch or two from the top of the glass and add half the heavy cream to each glass. Mix carefully with your long-handled spoon!

3 Now top with whipped cream and a cherry! You've got yourself one amazing egg cream (or two)!

> Make it a float by adding a scoop of ice cream instead of ice—perfect for celebrating your time together!

> Swap in cream soda instead of club soda.

> Try using caramel sauce instead of chocolate sauce.

Sheet Pan FAJITAS

Makes 4 servings ★ Prep time: 10 minutes ★ Cook time: 25 to 30 minutes

This is a fast and fun dinner for your whole family! Yummy tortillas stuffed with delicious chicken and veggies. Whenever raw meat is involved, it's very important that you and your helper both wash your hands any time you've touched it.

Equipment

Large mixing bowl
Small mixing bowl
Sheet pan
Spatula

Ingredients

For the Filling

3 to 4 chicken breasts
1 teaspoon garlic powder
1 teaspoon kosher salt
1 teaspoon paprika
½ teaspoon chili powder
½ teaspoon ground cumin
¼ teaspoon black pepper
2 tablespoons olive oil
1 red bell pepper
1 yellow bell pepper
1 green bell pepper
1 medium-size red onion
12 flour tortillas

For the Toppings

1 head iceberg lettuce, shredded
1 cup tomatoes, chopped
1¼ cups cheddar cheese, shredded
1 (12-ounce) jar salsa
1 (8-ounce) container sour cream

1 With a grown-up's help, preheat the oven to 425°F. Have your helper cut the chicken as thinly as they can—we are talking ¼-inch slices. Once all the chicken is sliced, ask them to put it in the large bowl while you mix up the seasoning! In the small bowl, mix up the garlic powder, salt, paprika, chili powder, ground cumin, and black pepper, and sprinkle it all right over the chicken. Then add the olive oil.

2 Ask an adult to help slice the peppers and onion as thinly as they sliced the chicken. Dump all those veggies into the bowl with the chicken. Here comes the fun part: mix it all up! Mix, mix, mix until every piece of chicken and every veggie is covered in our yummy seasoning!

3 Next up, pour all the chicken and veggies onto your baking sheet. Spread them out evenly, and then your helper can put the whole pan into the oven. Roast for 15 minutes, then have an adult use the spatula to flip everything over and continue cooking for at least another 10 minutes.

4 While the meat and veggies are in the oven, set the table with your topping station! Put each topping into its own bowl. You, my little chef, will taste test along the way to make sure things are perfect!

5 Once the fajitas are all perfectly cooked, it's time to eat! Place a tortilla on your plate and scoop the chicken and veggies right onto it. Never touch the hot pan, remember! Top with everything you love, from crunchy lettuce and melty cheese to sour cream and salsa! Fold it in half or roll it up—how you eat it is up to you!

Warm up the tortillas before you eat by wrapping them in a damp paper towel and microwaving for 10 seconds.

Any leftover fajita filling makes an incredible addition to scrambled eggs or next-day quesadillas.

Add other vegetables, like zucchini or broccoli.

The guacamole from snack time is an excellent topping!

No chicken? Use sirloin steak and reduce the baking time by 10 minutes.

Sizzling BEEF and BROCCOLI

Makes 4 servings ★ Prep time: 10 minutes ★ Cook time: 15 minutes

Pull up a chair and wash those hands! Dinner is about to be served (I bet your family is looking forward to this)!

Equipment

Large skillet
Spatula
Medium-size pan with lid
Plate

Ingredients

12 ounces (about 2 cups)
    sirloin steak
½ medium-size white onion
3 cups small broccoli florets
1 tablespoon olive oil
½ cup teriyaki sauce
1 tablespoon soy sauce
1 garlic clove, crushed and
    chopped
3 to 4 cups prepared plain rice

1 Ask an adult to heat the skillet on the stove over medium heat. They can slice up the meat and onion super thin while you carefully slice the broccoli florets in half!

2 Now that the skillet is hot, add the oil and your helper will add the meat. Cook it up until the meat is nice and tender and cooked just how you like it. Then ask an adult to remove the meat from the skillet onto a plate and set aside.

3 Add the broccoli to the medium-size pan with 2 cups of water. Put the lid on and cook over medium-high heat for 5 to 6 minutes. Then ask your helper to drain it!

4 Add the sliced onion, broccoli, and steak back to the pan with the teriyaki sauce, soy sauce, and garlic! Cook 3 to 4 minutes, and serve over rice!

When you have raw meat around, try not to touch it with your bare hands. If you do, wash your hands with soap so you don't spread germs.

Try using chicken!

Make a well in the center of the pan with the rice and veggies and crack an egg into it, then stir till fully cooked. Mix everything together for tasty fried rice!

Add more vegetables!

CHICKEN MEATBALL SLIDERS
(Mini Burgers)

Makes 24 (1-ounce) meatballs ★ Prep time: 10 minutes ★ Cook time: 15 to 20 minutes

Equipment

Box grater

Mixing bowl

Fork or wooden spoon

Lever-release ice cream scoop

Plate or baking sheet

12-inch skillet

Ingredients

For the Burgers

1 medium-size zucchini

1½ pounds ground meat

14 crackers, crushed (or ½ cup
    bread crumbs)

4 ounces Parmesan cheese, grated

1 egg

1 tablespoon olive oil

1 teaspoon onion powder

1 teaspoon garlic powder

Salt and pepper to taste

2 tablespoons olive oil for the
    frying pan

For the Fixins

12 mini slider buns or dinner rolls

12 lettuce leaves

12 pickle slices

6 cheese slices, folded in half

Ketchup

Mustard

1 Have an adult help you grate the zucchini! Take care not to scrape your fingers.

2 Put all the burger ingredients into the mixing bowl. Use a fork or big wooden spoon to mix it all up.

3 Once the meat mixture is all mixed up, grab your ice cream scoop! The ice cream scoop has a lever on it that makes for easy, even scooping. Using the scoop, measure the meat into 24 meatballs. It's okay if they aren't perfectly round—they will taste delicious! Set the uncooked meatballs on a plate or a baking sheet.

4 Have your helper heat the oil in a skillet over medium heat. Then they can carefully add the meat to the pan. You should be able to fit about 12 meatballs at a time. Count them out! Ask your grown-up to help fry the meatballs for 6 to 7 minutes, turning occasionally, until they are golden brown on all sides and cooked through.

5 To assemble your miniature burger, you will need your imagination! Are you ready? Put a meatball or two on your bun and then add everything else you love! Ketchup or mustard? Sure! Lettuce, cheese, and pickles? Go for it! Do you like it plain? That's good too! Remember, the best cooks are adventurous, so put on your adventure hat and try new foods!

Use ground turkey, pork, lamb, or beef.

Serve with veggies, chips, or any kind of fries you love!

Use any style of cheese you love as a topping!

No buns? No worries! Slice the meatballs in half and fold them into a slice of sandwich bread.

Want these gluten free? Substitute your favorite gluten-free crackers in the meat mixture.

French Dip SANDWICHES

Makes 4 servings ★ Prep time: 10 minutes ★ Bake time: 15 minutes

Equipment

Saucepan

Small bowl

Rubber spatula

Baking sheet

Parchment paper

4 small bowls

4 plates

Ingredients

3 cups low-sodium beef stock

½ yellow onion, chopped

1 teaspoon beef bouillon base

4 French rolls or 1 baguette, sliced in half

¼ cup mayonnaise

1 tablespoon mustard

4 slices cheddar cheese

12 ounces sliced deli roast beef

1 Put the beef stock, chopped onion, and bouillon in the saucepan and ask a grown-up to heat over medium. Simmer for 15 minutes while you prepare the sandwiches.

2 In a small bowl, mix the mayonnaise and mustard together, then spread just a bit on the top and bottom inside of every roll.

3 Divide the roast beef among the four rolls, and top each with one slice of cheese. Cover the baking sheet with parchment paper and place the rolls on it. Bake 10 to 15 minutes until the cheese is nice and melty and the roll is oh-so-toasty! Have an adult remove the sandwiches from the oven and put each sandwich on a plate.

4 Pour the beef broth into the small bowls. Dip the warm Frenchy dippy sammie into the warm beef broth. Mm-mmm!

Serve along with some crunchy chips and sliced veggies such as carrot sticks and sugar snap pea pods!

Use chicken stock in place of beef stock.

Use any deli meat you'd like! Change it up.

Chicken TORTELLINI SOUP

Makes 4 servings ★ Prep time: 10 minutes ★ Cook time: 15 to 20 minutes

Equipment

Stock pot
A big appetite!

Ingredients

2 (32-ounce) cartons
(8 cups) chicken stock
2 celery ribs, chopped
2 carrots, chopped
1 small yellow onion, chopped
1 chicken breast, sliced as
thinly as possible
½ teaspoon black pepper
Kosher salt to taste
1 16-ounce package fresh,
prepared cheese tortellini
pasta

1 Add the chicken stock, veggies, and chicken breast to the soup pot. Ask a grown-up to turn the heat to medium and bring everything to a simmer. Cook about 10 to 15 minutes.

2 Once the chicken is cooked through and veggies are tender, season with pepper and salt and carefully add the tortellini. Careful not to splash—the soup is hot! Cook 3 to 5 minutes. They cook extra fast because they are fresh. Serve with bread and butter and a nice big salad. Yes, chef!

Use any fresh stuffed pasta such as ravioli or unstuffed pasta, if you wish!

Skip the meat for a noodle-y delight!

Use vegetable broth, if you prefer!

Add more veggies or anything else you love!

Inside-Out CREAMY STUFFED SHELLS with TURKEY and BROCCOLI

Makes 6-8 servings ★ Prep time: 20 minutes ★ Bake time: 30 minutes

Broccoli gets a much-deserved dressing-up in this cheesy, yummy, tummy-approved pasta bake! The broccoli packs a vitamin punch and tastes like mac 'n' cheese with our creamy cheese sauce! Why inside out? When you stir all the filling ingredients together with the shells, it looks like the filling fell out!

Equipment

Stock pot
Slotted spoon
1 cup measuring cup
Colander
9-x-13 casserole dish

Ingredients

2 tablespoons butter
2 cups broccoli florets
8 to 10 ounces large shell pasta
    (a little over half a box)
1 pound ground turkey
1 garlic clove, smashed
Salt and pepper to taste
¼ cup flour
4 cups milk
3 cups cheddar cheese,
    shredded
½ cup Parmesan, shredded
1 cup pasta cooking water

1. Use 1 tablespoon of butter to grease your 9-x-13 casserole dish. Smear that butter into every corner!

2. Let's blanch the broccoli flowers! This means we are giving them a quick dip into boiling water to cook them slightly. Bring a large pot of water to a boil, and very gently drop in those broccoli florets with a grown-up's help. Let them cook for 3 minutes. Set a kitchen timer and sing a song while you wait! Adult helpers, this one's for you: using a slotted spoon, get all the broccoli out of the boiling water.

3. Add the shells to the same pot the broccoli was blanched in. Cook them in boiling water for 2 minutes less than the package instructions. Have an adult remove one cup of the cooking water and set it aside. (The easiest way is to dip a measuring cup with a handle right into the water.) Drain the shells and set aside.

4. Now that the pot is empty, use it to make your meaty and cheesy sauce! Ask your helper to set the burner temperature to medium. Add 1 tablespoon of butter to the pan. Brown the ground turkey until it's completely cooked, about 7 to 10 minutes. Halfway through, add the garlic. Season with salt and pepper. Ask a grown-up to show you just how much salt and pepper to add! Now, add the flour and stir it around the pot for 3 to 4 minutes. Next, in goes the milk. It's time to stir the pot and wait for the sauce to thicken. Add the broccoli and cheese! Stir, stir, stir!

5 Once the cheese is melted, add the shells. This is the best part! All that cheese sauce is filling the shells as you stir! If you need the sauce to be a little smoother or creamier, just add a little of the reserved pasta water ¼ cup at a time.

6 Pour the mixture into the buttered casserole dish. Top with more shredded cheese, if you'd like! Cover with foil and bake for 30 minutes. Ask a grown-up to remove the pan from the oven, then give each other a big hug and enjoy your cozy meal!

Use any ground meat you'd like! Chicken is great! Don't want meat? Skip it!

Want a crunchy top? Simply melt 2 tablespoons of butter mixed with 1 cup seasoned bread crumbs and sprinkle over the top of the shells before you bake it!

"Floret" sounds like the word flower, doesn't it? Well, the broccoli we eat IS the flower part of the broccoli plant! Each of those teeny, green buds will become a flower if it keeps growing. The larger piece of broccoli is called a crown—but it would look silly on your head, so it's best to put it in your tummy!

Feel free to add any green veggies. Peas and spinach work great!

This can be made 2 days ahead of time and even frozen for up to 1 week before you bake it!

Simply SWEDISH MEATBALLS and MASHERS

Makes 4 servings ★ Prep time: 20 minutes ★ Cook time: 10 minutes

This recipe has lots of parts, so it's very important that you let your grown-up helper take the lead! Scrub your hands with soap and warm water and let's get cookin'!

Equipment

Big stock pot
Big mixing bowl
Big spoon or rubber spatula
Levered ice cream scoop
Tongs
Paper towel–lined plate
Potato masher

Ingredients

For the Potatoes

8 large Yukon gold potatoes
   (skins on), quartered
½ cup butter
1½ cups whole milk
1 cup heavy cream
½ teaspoon kosher salt
¼ teaspoon black pepper

For the Meatballs

1 pound ground beef
½ pound ground pork or sausage
½ cup bread crumbs or crackers,
   finely crushed
¼ cup whole milk
¼ cup Parmesan cheese, grated
1 egg
1 teaspoon garlic powder
1 teaspoon onion powder
½ teaspoon kosher salt
¼ teaspoon black pepper
Olive oil for frying

For the Sauce

12 tablespoons of butter
2 to 3 tablespoons flour
2 cups chicken stock, plus more
   if needed
2 cups heavy cream
Salt and pepper to taste

1 Put all the potatoes into the big pot, cover them with cool water, and set the pot on the stove. Ask a grown-up to turn the heat on high and bring the water to a boil. Reduce the heat to medium-low and let the potatoes gently bubble away. Cook for 30 minutes, or until you can easily pierce the potato with a fork.

2 While the potatoes are cooking, put all the meatball ingredients except the oil into a big mixing bowl. Mix it all up with the big spoon or rubber spatula! If your arms get tired, I bet your helper would love to help. Use the ice cream scoop to measure out 16 to 20 meatballs that are about the size of a golf ball (approximately 2 tablespoons). Stop for a hand-washing break! Then ask an adult to heat a skillet and fry the meatballs in olive oil over medium heat, turning occasionally until they are nice and golden brown, about 10 minutes. Once the meatballs are done cooking, have a grown-up take them out of the skillet with tongs and set them aside on a plate lined with paper towels.

3 Once the 30-minute timer is up, ask your helper to drain the potatoes. Add the butter, milk, cream, salt, and pepper reserved for the potatoes to the pot. Use a hand masher to smash 'em all up! Lumpy is quite delicious!

4 While you mash, an adult is going to make the sauce. Ask your helper to melt 2 tablespoons of butter into the juices of the same pan you fried the meatballs in over medium heat. Stir in 2 tablespoons of flour to make a paste. Add the chicken stock and 2 cups of cream and stir over medium heat until smooth and combined. If it's too thick, add a bit more chicken broth or cream. Season with salt and pepper, and add the cooked meatballs to the sauce. Gently stir. Scoop some mashers onto a plate, spoon the meatballs and sauce over the top, and serve!

Skip the bread crumbs for gluten-free meatballs.

Add onions and mushrooms to your cream sauce for extra yummy flavor.

Use ground chicken or turkey instead of pork or sausage for the meatballs if you'd like.

Add 1 cup finely chopped spinach to your meatball mixture.

Serve your favorite green vegetable alongside (like garlicky green beans)!

Chicky TORTILLA ROLL-UPS (Flautas)

Makes 12 roll-ups ★ Prep time: 10 minutes ★ Bake time: 20 minutes

Crispy, creamy, crunchy dinnertime!

Equipment

Baking sheet
Parchment paper
Mixing bowl
Cutting board
Pastry brush

Ingredients

8 ounces cream cheese,
   softened
½ cup salsa
1 cup cheddar cheese,
   shredded
1 teaspoon onion powder
1 teaspoon paprika
1 teaspoon garlic powder
Salt and pepper to taste
4 cups chicken, shredded
   (Rotisserie chicken works
   amazing!)
12 soft taco-size flour tortillas
4 tablespoons (½ stick)
   butter, melted

1 Have a grown-up preheat the oven to 375°F. Line your baking sheet with parchment paper.

2 In your mixing bowl, mix up the cream cheese, salsa, cheddar cheese, seasonings, and salt and pepper until it's all combined. Fold the chicken into the mixture.

3 Put 2 to 3 tablespoons of your chicken mixture in the center of each tortilla and flatten it down on the cutting board. Roll up the tortilla tightly around the filling. It will look like a little flute, also known as a flauta! Place it on your baking sheet seam-side down.

4 Repeat this process until you've rolled up all the tortillas, then brush each one with the melted butter. Bake 25 minutes until they are golden brown and crisp.

Serve with
sour cream,
salsa, or
guacamole
for dipping.

Use any
meat you love:
ground beef,
shredded beef,
or turkey.

Make a big
green salad and
chomp on crunchy
lettuce alongside
your flautas.

Cheesy MEXICAN RICE

Makes 4 servings ★ Prep time: 3 to 4 minutes ★ Cook time: 15 minutes

Equipment

Large saucepan with lid
Wooden spoon
Fork
A hungry belly

Ingredients

1 cup jasmine rice

1 tablespoon olive oil

½ teaspoon onion powder

½ teaspoon paprika

½ teaspoon turmeric

½ teaspoon kosher salt

2 garlic cloves, smashed and
    chopped

2 cups chicken stock

1 cup cheddar cheese,
    shredded

1 Place the dry rice, oil, and seasonings into your saucepan, and have an adult turn the heat to medium. Toast the rice until it smells delicious, stirring often, about 3 minutes. Then add the garlic and cook for just a minute.

2 Pour the chicken stock into the pan and bring it to a bubbling boil over high heat, about 2 minutes. Now ask your helper to turn it down to low. Put the lid on the saucepan and set a timer for 15 minutes.

3 When the timer goes off, remove the pan from the heat and add the cheese! Fluff the rice and cheese with a fork. Serve it up, chef!

Add ½ cup salsa to the finished rice for a spicy treat.

Add a pound of ground meat to the rice in the very beginning for a complete, tasty meal!

Add 1 cup chopped veggies at the beginning for added fun and flavor (plus nutrition)!

Grannie's SPECIAL CREAMED CORN

Makes 4 servings ★ Prep time: 15 minutes ★ Cook time: 15 minutes

Equipment

Large bowl
Tiny bowl
Large skillet
Wooden spoon

Ingredients

5 ears of corn
1 tablespoon butter
Salt and pepper to taste
1 cup heavy cream
½ cup Parmesan, shredded

1 Place the small bowl upside down inside the big bowl. Looks silly, but wait till you see this trick! Have an adult stand a corn cob on its end atop the upside-down bowl and slice the corn off the cob. The big bowl catches all those kernels! Repeat with each ear of corn.

2 Melt the butter in the skillet over medium heat. Let a grown-up help because it's hot!

3 Add the corn to the skillet and gently stir. This is the perfect time to season with salt and pepper!

4 Add the cream and Parmesan cheese, then cook until it's thick and bubbly. My little chef friend, you just made fresh, delicious creamed corn.

Use any veggies you love. This recipe works wonderfully with spinach, peas, and even zucchini!

Garlicky GREEN BEANS

Makes 4 servings ★ Prep time: 5 minutes ★ Cook time: 10 minutes

Equipment

Large skillet with lid
Colander
Wooden spoon

Ingredients

1 tablespoon kosher salt
4 cups green beans, trimmed
2 tablespoons butter
2 garlic cloves, minced
Black pepper to taste

1 Grab that skillet! Have an adult put it on the stove and turn the heat on to medium-high.

2 Fill the skillet with 2 inches of water and add the salt. Carefully add the green beans to the water—try not to splash!—and put a lid on the skillet. Simmer 7 minutes. You have to let that water get all bubbly to cook the beans!

3 Ask your helper to drain the beans into the colander, then put them back in the pan. Now you can add the butter, garlic, and pepper! Sauté, or fry quickly in the hot fat, 2 to 3 minutes more, stirring occasionally with your wooden spoon. Don't overcook your beans! A perfectly cooked bean should still have a bit of a crunch when you bite into it. Serve up alongside your favorite dinner!

This method works for a number of vegetables such as broccoli, brussels sprouts, cauliflower or carrots!

Buttery STEAMED BROCCOLI

Makes 4 servings ★ Prep time: 5 minutes ★ Cook time: 6 minutes

These are so fun and simple and look like delicious buttery TREES!

Equipment
Skillet with lid
Spatula

Ingredients
3 cups fresh broccoli florets
2 to 3 tablespoons butter
Salt and pepper to taste

1 Ask a grown-up to bring one inch of water to a simmer in your skillet over medium-high heat. Add the broccoli and place the lid on the skillet. Set a timer for 6 minutes. Watch those tiny trees turn bright green!

2 Ask an adult to drain any water off after 6 minutes and put the broccoli back inside the hot pan. Cook the broccoli for 1 minute to get ALL the water out. Now, melt the butter into the pan, and they're ready to munch on!

Use this recipe for cauliflower too!

Sprinkle ½ cup shredded cheddar cheese over the top of the broccoli for a cheesy delight!

Add a smashed garlic clove to the butter for extra yummy flavor.

Chocolate Chip Cookie
ICE CREAM SANDWICHES

Makes 6 servings ★ Prep time: 30 minutes ★ Bake time: 12 minutes ★ Assembly time: 15 minutes

Who doesn't love a good chocolate chip cookie? And who doesn't flip for ice cream sandwiches? We are going to make the very best chocolate chip cookie ice cream sandwiches ever! Make sure those hands are clean and pull your stool up to the counter.

Equipment
Mixing bowl
Wooden spoon
Cookie sheet

Ingredients
½ cup packed brown sugar
½ cup white sugar
½ cup plus 1 tablespoon butter, softened
1 extra-large egg
1 teaspoon vanilla extract
¼ teaspoon kosher salt
1¼ cup flour
½ teaspoon baking soda
1½ cups dark chocolate chips
1 pint (2 cups) vanilla ice cream

1. Ask a grown-up to preheat the oven to 375°F.

2. Measure out the sugars and butter into a bowl, then mix like the wind! Once the butter and sugar looks nice and creamy, add the egg, vanilla, and salt. Mix! Add the flour, baking soda, and chocolate chips. Have an adult help mix up this part if your arms are getting tired!

3. Set the cookie batter into the fridge for a quick chill, about 15 to 20 minutes.

4. Oh boy, it's time to scoop! Scoop out 12 big, even cookie dough balls onto your cookie sheet. Make sure to leave plenty of room between each cookie dough ball because they will spread out! Have your helper put the pan in the oven and bake 12 minutes. Take the vanilla ice cream out of the freezer and put it on the counter to soften while the cookies bake. Then let a grown-up take the pan out of the oven and allow the cookies to cool on the baking sheet.

5. Now, it's time to make the sandwiches! Scoop a big spoonful of softened vanilla ice cream onto the flat side of one cookie, then top with another cookie! You can assemble the other 5 sammies and enjoy them now, soft and squishy, or freeze them for later!

Use any kind of ice cream you'd like!

Add ½ cup chopped walnuts to your cookie batter for a nutty surprise!

Want a double chocolate cookie? Swap ¼ cup flour out for ¼ cup unsweetened cocoa powder.

To save these, wrap them individually in parchment paper and put each one in a zip-closure sandwich bag. They will last 7 to 10 days in the freezer.

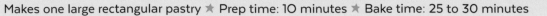

STRAWBERRY "Toaster" PASTRY

Makes one large rectangular pastry ★ Prep time: 10 minutes ★ Bake time: 25 to 30 minutes

Equipment

Rolling pin
Parchment paper
Baking sheet
Two small mixing bowls
Fork

Ingredients

For the Pastry

A little flour for dusting your
    workstation
1 box frozen rolled pie crusts
(2 crusts), thawed
1 cup strawberry jam
1 cup strawberries, chopped

For the Glaze

1½ cups confectioners' sugar
2 tablespoons strawberry jam
1 tablespoon lemon juice

1 Have a grown-up preheat the oven to 350°F. Now, sprinkle a little flour on your workstation—that's just a fancy word for the counter or table.

2 Carefully unroll the pie crust dough, and use the rolling pin to help you roll and push the bottom pie crust into a rectangle shape a little smaller than your baking sheet—it doesn't have to be perfect. Now lay it on a parchment paper–lined baking sheet.

3 Mix the jam and chopped strawberries together in a bowl and spread the mixture all over the bottom crust.

4 Roll and shape the second pie crust into roughly the same kind of rectangle as the bottom crust. Lay it across the top of the fruit and jam mixture. Here comes the fun part! Press all the edges together with a fork, and poke several holes all over the top for steam to escape! Bake 25 to 30 minutes. Allow to cool.

5 Let's mix up the glaze! Combine the sugar, jam, and lemon juice in a bowl. Use a spoon to drizzle it all over the pastry. Then cut into squares, and you're ready to eat!

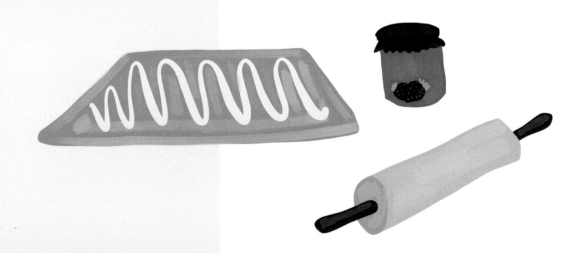

BANANA CAKE with CREAM CHEESE FROSTING

Makes about 12 servings ★ Prep time: 15 minutes ★ Bake time: 25 to 35 minutes

Move over, banana bread—banana CAKE is here! It's light and fluffy with the yummiest frosting, perfect for celebrating every day you're with the ones you love!

Equipment

2 large mixing bowls
Wooden spoon
9-x-13 cake pan
Hand mixer

Ingredients

For the Cake

2 to 3 tablespoons butter, chilled
4 ripe bananas (with brown spots, please! Brown spots mean a banana is extra sweet!)
⅓ cup vanilla or plain yogurt
1 cup dark brown sugar
½ cup granulated sugar
½ cup butter, melted
2 eggs
2 tablespoons oil
2 teaspoons vanilla extract
1¾ cups flour
1 teaspoon baking powder
½ teaspoon baking soda
½ teaspoon kosher salt
½ teaspoon cinnamon

For the Frosting

8 ounces cream cheese, softened
3 cups powdered sugar
½ cup butter, softened
½ teaspoon vanilla extract
Pinch of salt

1 Butter your 9-x-13 baking dish with the chilled butter. You can use your fingers to squish the butter into the corners! Just remember to wash your hands after you're done.

2 Ask a grown-up to preheat the oven to 350°F. Peel the bananas, dump them into the mixing bowl, and smash 'em up real good with a fork. Next, add the yogurt, sugars, melted butter, eggs, oil, and vanilla into your bowl and mix like the wind!

3 Next, dump in that flour, baking powder, baking soda, salt, and cinnamon. Mix everything up until just combined—no overmixing!

4 Pour the batter (with an adult's help) into your baking dish and bake 25 to 35 minutes until it's golden brown and cooked all the way through. Ask your helper to take the cake out of the oven to cool while you make the frosting.

5 Add the frosting ingredients to a clean mixing bowl. Gently, on low speed, mix all the ingredients until smooth. Careful now, powdered sugar loves to fly around the kitchen if you go too fast! Once your cake is completely cool, frost it up!

Skip the frosting if you'd like!

For chocolate banana cake, in place of the 1¾ cups of flour, substitute 1½ cups flour and ⅓ cup unsweetened cocoa powder.

Add ½ cup chopped walnuts for extra crunch.

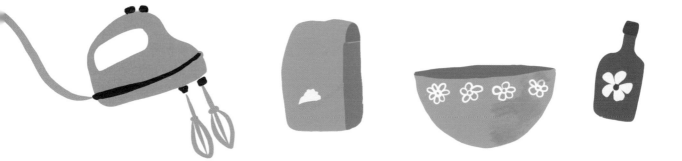

Very Berry SHORT CRUST COBBLER

Makes about 12 servings ★ Prep time: 20 minutes ★ Bake time: 35 to 45 minutes

Is there anything as tasty as a slice of pie? A fruity cobbler! Think of cobbler as pie's cousin or best friend. Or a cousin who's also a best friend! It's deliciously sweetened fruit with a crumbly, buttery top. Wash your hands and grab a chair or stool!

Equipment

2 large mixing bowls
Wooden spoon
9-x-13 glass baking dish

Ingredients

For the Filling

2 cups strawberries, diced
2 cups blueberries
1 cup raspberries
3 to 4 teaspoons cornstarch
Pinch of salt
1 to 2 cups sugar, depending on
   how sweet your fruit is, plus
      2 tablespoons
1 tablespoon butter

For the Crust

1 cup butter, softened
1½ cups flour
½ cup granulated sugar
Pinch of salt

1 Ask a grown-up to preheat the oven to 350°F.

2 Let's prepare the fruit filling! In a large mixing bowl, dump all of the filling ingredients except the butter and 2 tablespoons of granulated sugar. Gently stir the fruit so you don't mash it up. Sooooo gentle! Grab your glass 9-x-13 baking dish and butter it up! Then sprinkle 2 tablespoons of granulated sugar in the bottom of the dish. Now shake, shake, shake that dish and swirl that sugar around. The sugar sticks to the butter to create a sugary, buttery nonstick surface. Pour the fruit in the baking dish.

3 Time for the crust! Put all crust ingredients in a clean mixing bowl. Using your wooden spoon, mix until it's nice and crumbly. This job can make your arm tired, so make sure to take turns with your helper. Just when you think you couldn't possibly stir for one more second, you are probably done! You want this dough to be fall-apart crumbly, but if you pinched it, it would stay together.

4 Let's put that cobbler together and get it cooking! Get your hands in there and sprinkle the crust crumbles all over the fruit. Bake uncovered 35 to 45 minutes or until it's bubbling and delicious. Allow to cool at least 10 to 15 minutes before digging in!

Serve with vanilla ice cream to make it à la mode!

Add ½ cup oats to the crumble dough to make it crisp!

Try peaches or apples for this recipe, as well! Any fruit works beautifully, except for bananas and melons. Those fruits don't love being made into cobblers.

If you choose to use apples or pears, add 1 teaspoon of cinnamon to the fruit.

No cornstarch? No problem. Use the same amount of flour. It won't be glossy, but it will thicken the fruit juices.

No fresh berries? Frozen fruit works just fine! They have more water in them, so don't worry if there's a bit more liquid. These are perfect for spooning over ice cream too.

Orange Creamsicle MILKSHAKES

Makes 4 servings ★ Prep time: 10 minutes

Equipment

Blender
Rubber spatula or spoon
Medium-size bowl
4 cups
An appetite for sweets

Ingredients

1 cup heavy cream

2 tablespoons sugar

8 ounces frozen orange juice concentrate (100% juice)

1 cup whole milk

2 cups (1 pint) vanilla ice cream

5 shortbread butter cookies, crushed

1 First up, let's make the blender whipped cream! Pour the heavy cream and sugar into your blender. Put the lid on top and ask a grown-up to help you blend on low 2 to 3 minutes, or until the cream looks slightly firm. If you turn off the blender and the cream stays in place, it's ready! Have your helper spoon the whipped cream into the bowl.

2 Next comes the milkshake itself! Add the orange juice concentrate, milk, and ice cream to the blender and blend on low 1 to 2 minutes.

3 Line up 4 cups and pour in the milkshake. Top with whipped cream and cookie crumbs. Enjoy!

Use any frozen juice concentrate to make any flavor of creamy, fruity milkshake.

Add a cherry on top—it's the perfect treat topper!

Make chocolate shakes by using chocolate syrup instead of orange juice concentrate.

Chocolate Peanut Butter "NICE" CREAM

Makes 2 to 3 cups ★ Prep time: 10 minutes

Ice cream is delightful, but not nearly as delightful as NICE CREAM!

Equipment

Food processor

Ingredients

4 frozen bananas

2 tablespoons unsweetened cocoa powder

¼ cup ice-cold milk

1 teaspoon vanilla extract

Pinch of salt

¼ cup peanut butter

2 tablespoons brown sugar

1 Plop all ingredients into the food processor. Put the lid on and ask a grown-up to help whirl it on low speed for 2 to 3 minutes until it's nice and ICE CREAMY! It will look like soft serve. Get a spoon and dig in!

Skip the chocolate and peanut butter for plain vanilla.

Add any other frozen fruit such as raspberries and peaches to the bananas for a delicious flavor combo.

Top with chopped nuts and chocolate sauce for a nice cream sundae! Actually, top it with ANYTHING YOU WANT! This is your creation—go nuts!

Double CHOCOLATE, Double DELICIOUS Crackly Top BROWNIES

★ Makes 9 brownies ★

Are you ready for the most scrumptious brownies you've ever tasted? Everyone will be asking to see your cape once they taste these chocolate treats because you are going to be a hero! Are your hands clean? Let's make dessert!

Equipment

Large mixing bowl

Measuring cup

Rubber spatula or wooden spoon

12-x-12-inch sheet of oven-safe parchment paper

9-x-9 square pan

A chocolaty appetite

Ingredients

½ cup butter, melted

½ cup vegetable oil

2 cups granulated sugar

1 teaspoon vanilla

½ teaspoon kosher salt

4 eggs

1 cup bittersweet chocolate, melted

½ cup unsweetened cocoa powder

1 cup flour

10 ounces milk chocolate, chopped

1 Ask a grown-up to preheat that oven to 350°F.

2 Little chef, get the spatula or wooden spoon ready—you are one amazing mixer! Add the melted butter and oil to the bowl, then add the sugar and mix like the wind! Add the vanilla and salt to the bowl and stir! You are cookin' now, chef!

3 Time to crack those eggs. Add the eggs to the bowl and mix to combine with the buttery sugar, but don't overmix them because they don't like it too much. If a little bit of the shell falls into in the batter, don't worry! You can use a bigger piece of the eggshell to fish out the tinier bit!

4 Add the melted chocolate and just *barely* mix it in. Add the cocoa powder and flour and stir until they have just disappeared, then add the chopped chocolate.

5 This is the best part! Lay the parchment paper into your 9-x-9 pan. While an adult holds the bowl of batter over the pan, you can scoop it out on the parchment. Use the rubber spatula to scrape the sides of the bowl and make sure every bit of batter makes it into the pan. Ask your helper to pop the pan into the oven. Stand back—it's hot!

6 Bake this chocolaty treat about 20 to 25 minutes. Great brownies have a bit of a wobbly center. Flip that oven light on and watch the magic happen! When the timer is done, ask a grown-up to remove the pan from the oven and let cool. Cut into squares, and enjoy!

Add nuts! Walnuts, almonds, hazelnuts...go nuts!

No chocolate? That's alright, just skip it! Your brownie will be a bit less fudgy. Bake 2 minutes less.

Want to try a blondie? Skip all the chocolate and swap in 1 cup brown sugar for 1 cup white sugar.

Add any baking chips you like: peanut butter, white chocolate, even candy-coated chocolates.

Key Lime Pie MILKSHAKES

Makes 4 servings ★ Prep time: 10 minutes

Blender sweets are possibly the most fun dessert EVER!

Equipment

Blender
Rubber spatula or spoon
A medium-size bowl
4 cups
A sweet tooth

Ingredients

1 cup heavy cream
2 tablespoons sugar
½ cup frozen limeade
   concentrate (100% juice)
½ cup half and half
2 cups (1 pint) vanilla
   ice cream
3 whole graham crackers,
   crushed

1 First up, we'll make the blender whipped cream! Pour the heavy cream into your blender and add the sugar. Put the lid on top and ask a grown-up to help you blend on low for 2 to 3 minutes, or until the cream looks slightly firm. If you turn off the blender, and the cream stays in place, you'll know it's done! Ask an adult to spoon the whipped cream into the bowl.

2 Add the limeade concentrate, half-and-half, and ice cream to the blender and blend on low 1 to 2 minutes.

3 Line up the cups and pour in the milkshake. Top with whipped cream and graham cracker crumbs. **DELICIOUS!**

> Use any flavor of frozen concentrate to change it up.

> Add a splash of maraschino cherry juice for cherry limeade!

> Make chocolate shakes by using chocolate syrup instead of limeade concentrate!

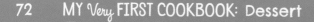

How did the jury find the hamburger?

Grillty as charred!

What is a toad's favorite type of soda?

Croak-a-Cola

What do rabbits say when they sit down for dinner?

"Lettuce eat."

How to you make an egg roll?

It's easy, you just push it!

Hee-hee!

Ha-ha!

What's worse than finding a worm in your apple?

Finding half a worm in your apple.

What is an egg's least favorite day of the week?

Fry-day, of course!

Where do hamburgers go to dance?

The meatball!

What do you get when you cross a monkey with a peach?

An ape-ricot!

What did the carrot say to the broccoli?

Nothing. Vegetables can't talk.

Is it proper to eat with your fingers?

No, you should eat with your mouth!

When potatoes have kids, what are they called?

Tater tots.

Hee-hee!

Ha-ha!

Daddy!

Why do fish swim in salt water?

Because pepper water would make them sneeze!

How do you make a milkshake?

Put a cow on a roller coaster.

Why couldn't the butter leave the casino?

Because it was on a roll!

What does a nut say when it sneezes?

"Cashew!"

What has ears but can't hear?

A cornfield!

What does bread wear to bed?

Jammies.

What do you call cheese when it's all by itself?

Provolone.

Let's CELEBRATE!

Every day can be special. It doesn't have to be a holiday or your birthday. YOU are special and that is a reason to celebrate! When we wake up each morning feeling grateful for the day, it gets very easy to have a heart for celebration.

Here are some ways you can celebrate:

Ask a loved one what their very favorite meal was when they were your age! Maybe you can make that meal together!

Ask a grown-up to take you fishing or on a hike!

Build a fort—out of wood, cardboard, pillows, you name it! Make it big enough for at least two people, so you can invite a loved one inside for a visit!

Play a game! Charades, hide-and-seek, tag, you name it! Just be sure to laugh a lot.

Bake a cake! Any day is a good day for cake!

Every once in a while, ask those in your family how their day is going. Maybe they need a hug or someone to talk to. Maybe they just want somebody to play a game with. You'd be the perfect person for all of it!

Get some loved ones together for a water balloon battle! Just be sure to do it outside on a warm day!

Go for a walk and spot all the different flowers and trees! Bring back a bouquet of the prettiest flowers. Or gather fallen leaves or interesting rocks

Visit the farmers market with an adult. I bet you can learn about all kinds of fruits and veggies you've never even seen before!

Paint a beautiful picture for someone special to you!

You are the perfect person to find the joy in the every day. At breakfast, lunchtime, snack time, dinnertime, or even dessert, talk about all the joyful moments together at the table.

Let's TALK!

When we're together sharing a meal or just having a snack, it's a great time to connect. Here are some questions for you to take turns asking each other to get your conversation going!

Let's make up a song! What should we sing about?

If you could be a superhero, what superpower would you have?

What do you like to read about?

If you could change anything about yourself, what would it be? Why?

What's your favorite memory with me so far?

What are you thankful for?

Who's your best friend? Why?

What is the one thing about yourself that you would never change? Why?

What's your favorite pizza topping?

If we could go to the beach today, what would you want to do first?

★ ★ WRITE YOUR *Very* OWN RECIPE ★ ★

Name: _____ Date: _____

Serves: _____ Prep Time: _____ Cook Time: _____

Equipment

_____

_____

_____

_____

_____

Ingredients

_____

_____

_____

_____

_____

_____

_____

_____

_____

Directions

_____

_____

_____

_____

_____

_____

_____

_____

_____

_____

_____

_____

_____

_____

_____

_____

Why I *love* it: _____

_____ ♥

★ ★ WRITE YOUR *Very* OWN RECIPE ★ ★

Name: _____ Date: _____

Serves: _____ Prep Time: _____ Cook Time: _____

Equipment

_____
_____
_____
_____
_____

Ingredients

_____
_____
_____
_____
_____
_____
_____
_____
_____

Directions

_____
_____
_____
_____
_____
_____
_____
_____
_____
_____
_____
_____
_____
_____
_____

Why I *love* it: _____
_____ ♥

★ ★ WRITE YOUR *Very* OWN RECIPE ★ ★

Name: _____ Date: _____

Serves: _____ Prep Time: _____ Cook Time: _____

Equipment

_____

_____

_____

_____

_____

Ingredients

_____

_____

_____

_____

_____

_____

_____

_____

_____

_____

Directions

_____

_____

_____

_____

_____

_____

_____

_____

_____

_____

_____

_____

_____

_____

_____

_____

Why I *love* it: _____

_____ ♥

★ ★ WRITE YOUR *Very* OWN RECIPE ★ ★

Name: _____ Date: _____

Serves: _____ Prep Time: _____ Cook Time: _____

Equipment

_____
_____
_____
_____
_____

Ingredients

_____
_____
_____
_____
_____
_____
_____
_____

Directions

_____
_____
_____
_____
_____
_____
_____
_____
_____
_____
_____
_____
_____
_____
_____

Why I *love* it: _____
_____ ♥

★ ★ WRITE YOUR *Very* OWN RECIPE ★ ★

Name: _____ Date: _____

Serves: _____ Prep Time: _____ Cook Time: _____

Equipment

_____

_____

_____

_____

_____

Ingredients

_____

_____

_____

_____

_____

_____

_____

_____

_____

_____

Directions

_____

_____

_____

_____

_____

_____

_____

_____

_____

_____

_____

_____

_____

_____

_____

_____

_____

Why I *love* it: _____

_____ ♥

★ ★ WRITE YOUR *Very* OWN RECIPE ★ ★

Name: _____ Date: _____

Serves: _____ Prep Time: _____ Cook Time: _____

Equipment

_____
_____
_____
_____
_____

Ingredients

_____
_____
_____
_____
_____
_____
_____

Directions

_____
_____
_____
_____
_____
_____
_____
_____
_____
_____
_____
_____
_____
_____

Why I *love* it: _____
_____ ♥

★ ★ WRITE YOUR *Very* OWN RECIPE ★ ★

Name: _____ Date: _____

Serves: _____ Prep Time: _____ Cook Time: _____

Equipment

_____

_____

_____

_____

_____

_____

Ingredients

_____

_____

_____

_____

_____

_____

_____

_____

_____

_____

Directions

_____

_____

_____

_____

_____

_____

_____

_____

_____

_____

_____

_____

_____

_____

_____

_____

_____

Why I *love* it: _____

_____ ♥

Name: _____ Date: _____

Serves: _____ Prep Time: _____ Cook Time: _____

Equipment

_____

_____

_____

_____

_____

Ingredients

_____

_____

_____

_____

_____

_____

_____

_____

_____

Directions

_____

_____

_____

_____

_____

_____

_____

_____

_____

_____

_____

_____

_____

_____

_____

Why I *love* it: _____

_____ ♥

★ ★ WRITE YOUR *Very* OWN RECIPE ★ ★

Name: _____ Date: _____

Serves: _____ Prep Time: _____ Cook Time: _____

Equipment

_____

_____

_____

_____

_____

Ingredients

_____

_____

_____

_____

_____

_____

_____

_____

_____

_____

Directions

_____

_____

_____

_____

_____

_____

_____

_____

_____

_____

_____

_____

_____

_____

_____

Why I *love* it: _____

_____ ♥

★ ★ WRITE YOUR *Very* OWN RECIPE ★ ★

Name: _____ Date: _____

Serves: _____ Prep Time: _____ Cook Time: _____

Equipment

_____
_____
_____
_____
_____
_____

Ingredients

_____
_____
_____
_____
_____
_____
_____
_____
_____

Directions

_____
_____
_____
_____
_____
_____
_____
_____
_____
_____
_____
_____
_____
_____
_____

Why I *love* it: _____
_____ ♥

★ ★ WRITE YOUR *Very* OWN RECIPE ★ ★

Name: _____ Date: _____

Serves: _____ Prep Time: _____ Cook Time: _____

Equipment

_____
_____
_____
_____
_____

Ingredients

_____
_____
_____
_____
_____
_____
_____
_____
_____
_____

Directions

_____
_____
_____
_____
_____
_____
_____
_____
_____
_____
_____
_____
_____
_____
_____
_____

Why I *love* it: _____
_____ ♥